WHAT MAKES AMERICA *America?*

TITLE LIST

The Northern Colonies: The Quest for Freedom (1600–1700)

The Southern Colonies: The Quest for Prosperity (1600–1700)

The Original United States of America:
Americans Discover the Meaning of Independence (1770–1800)

Thomas Jefferson's America: The Louisiana Purchase (1800–1811)

The Expanding United States: The Rise of Nationalism (1812–1820)

A Proud and Isolated Nation: Americans Take a Stand in Texas (1820–1845)

From Sea to Shining Sea: Americans Move West (1846–1860)

Americans Divided: The Civil War (1860–1865)

What the Land Means to Americans: Alaska and Other Wilderness Areas (1865–1890)

Crossing the Seas: Americans Form an Empire (1890–1899)

A World Contender: Americans on the Global Stage (1900–1912)

Super Power: Americans Today

What Makes America America?

WHAT MAKES AMERICA *America?*

BY

ERIC SCHWARTZ

MASON CREST PUBLISHERS

PHILADELPHIA

Mason Crest Publishers Inc.
370 Reed Road
Broomall, Pennsylvania 19008
(866) MCP-BOOK (toll free)

First printing
1 2 3 4 5 6 7 8 9 10

Library of Congress Cataloging-in-Publication Data

Schwartz, Eric.
What makes America America? / by Eric Schwartz.
p. cm.
ISBN 1-59084-913-2 ISBN 1-59084-900-0 (series)
1. United States—Civilization—Juvenile literature. 2. National characteristics, American—Juvenile literature. 3. United States—Politics and government—Juvenile literature. 4. United States—Politics and government—Sources—Juvenile literature. I. Title.
E169.1.S384 2004
973—dc22

2004009439

Design by Dianne Hodack.
Produced by Harding House Publishing Service, Inc.
Cover design by Dianne Hodack.
Printed in the Hashemite Kingdom of Jordan.

CONTENTS

Introduction

by Dr. Jack Rakove

Today's America is not the same geographical shape as the first American colonies—and the concept of America has evolved as well over the years.

When the thirteen original states declared their independence from Great Britain, most Americans still lived within one or two hours modern driving time from the Atlantic coast. In other words, the Continental Congress that approved the Declaration of Independence on July 4, 1776, was continental in name only. Yet American leaders like George Washington, Benjamin Franklin, and Thomas Jefferson also believed that the new nation did have a continental destiny. They expected it to stretch at least as far west as the Mississippi River, and they imagined that it could extend even further. The framers of the Federal Constitution of 1787 provided that western territories would join the Union on equal terms with the original states. In 1803, President Jefferson brought that continental vision closer to reality by purchasing the vast Louisiana Territory from France. In the 1840s, negotiations with Britain and a war with Mexico brought the United States to the Pacific Ocean.

This expansion created great opportunities, but it also brought serious costs. As Americans surged westward, they created a new economy of family farms and large plantations. But between the Ohio River and the Gulf of Mexico, expansion also brought the continued growth of plantation slavery for millions of African Americans. Political struggle over the extension of slavery west of the Mississippi was one of the major causes of the Civil War that killed hundreds of thousands of Americans in the 1860s but ended with the destruction of slavery. Creating opportunities for American farmers also meant displacing Native Americans from the lands their ancestors had occupied for centuries. The opening of the west encouraged massive immigration not only from Europe but also from Asia, as Chinese workers came to labor in the California Gold Rush and the building of the railroads.

By the end of the nineteenth century, Americans knew that their great age of territorial expansion was over. But immigration and the growth of modern industrial cities continued to change the American landscape. Now Americans moved back and forth across the continent in search of economic opportunities. African Americans left the South in massive numbers and settled in dense concentrations in the cities of the North. The United States remained a magnet for immigration, but new immigrants came increasingly from Mexico, Central America, and Asia.

Ever since the seventeenth century, expansion and migration across this vast landscape have shaped American history. These books are designed to explain how this process has worked. They tell the story of how modern America became the nation it is today.

"It is to secure our rights that we resort to government at all."
–Thomas Jefferson

Thomas Jefferson

One
THE DECLARATION OF INDEPENDENCE

Over the past 230 years, much about America has changed. The United States has extended its borders far past the dreams of the original American settlers. Modern inventions, current events, and twenty-first-century ideas have all changed the way Americans think about their nation.

But some things have not changed. At the very core of the United States are important concepts that not only shaped the nation at its birth, but that continue to shape it today. Many of these ideas are expressed in documents and laws that form a foundation for the American systems of law and government. The Declaration of Independence is perhaps the earliest stone in this foundation.

THE HISTORY OF THE DECLARATION OF INDEPENDENCE

Almost exactly fifty years after the signing of the Declaration of Independence and ten days before his death, Thomas Jefferson wrote his last letter, respectfully declining an invitation to attend a special Fourth of July celebration in Philadelphia. His health failing fast, Jefferson nonetheless wished that he could attend. His letter described how he valued the Declaration of Independence, which showed "that the mass of mankind has not been born with saddles on their backs, nor a favored few booted and spurred, ready to ride them legitimately, by the grace of God."

The Declaration of Independence borrowed many of its words and ideas from other sources. Jefferson himself acknowledged from the first that the Declaration of Independence was not a solo act nor statement of new political ideas. As he put it in a letter to his friend Richard Henry Lee:

> Neither aiming at originality of principle or sentiment, nor yet copied from any particular and previous writing, it was intended to be an expression of the American mind, and to give to that expression the proper tone and spirit called for by the occasion. All its authority rests then on the harmonizing sentiments of the day, whether expressed in conversation, in letters, printed essays or in the elementary books of public right, as Aristotle, Cicero, Locke, Sidney, etc.

Indeed, it would have been hard to persuade the Continental Congress gathering in Philadelphia that year to approve a declaration of original ideas. Only a year earlier, in fact, a majority of ***delegates*** still clung to the belief that the union between the colonies and Great Britain could be mended. In January 1776, only seven men in Congress were in favor of independence.

Signing of the Declaration of Independence

Fast Facts

DECLARATION OF INDEPENDENCE

Who wrote the Declaration?
Thomas Jefferson

When was it written?
July 4, 1776

Where was it written?
Philadelphia, Pennsylvania

Who signed it? Delegates from all thirteen American colonies.

Why was it written? To explain to the world why the colonists needed to separate from Great Britain.

Samuel Adams, who probably has the most ***radical*** reputation of any of the colonial leaders, signed instructions to the delegates to the First Continental Congress in 1774 that "harmony between Great Britain and the colonies" was "most ardently desired by all good men." Benjamin Franklin declared in March 1775, that he had never heard arguments for independence in the colonies "from any person, drunk or sober."

But the situation was changing rapidly in 1776. The battles of Lexington and Concord were fought in April 1775, and in August 1775 a royal proclamation declared that the King's American subjects were "engaged in open and avowed rebellion." ***Parliament*** responded by passing the American Prohibitory Act, forbidding trade with America and allowing captured ships to be treated as enemy property.

By the spring of 1776, it was clear to many that the colonies must formally declare their independence from Great Britain. The Privateering Resolution, passed in March 1776 by the Continental Congress, effectively encouraged colonists to outfit their own ships to attack "enemies of these United Colonies." In April, American ports were opened to commerce with countries besides Great Britain, severing the previous economic ties with the motherland. In May, the Continental Congress passed a "Resolution for the Formation of Local Governments."

THE IDEAS BEHIND THE DECLARATION OF INDEPENDENCE

Mixed with this recognition of the need for independence was the belief that the new nation must also embody ***democratic principles***. The thinking of many people was shaped by the best-selling

Independence Hall

Delegates *are people who act for others as representatives.*

Radical *means marked by considerable difference from the usual or traditional.*

Parliament *is the nobility, clergy, and commoners called together by the British sovereign as the supreme legislative body in the United Kingdom.*

Democratic principles *are the code of conduct or rules of a government by the people.*

pamphlet *Common Sense,* written by Thomas Paine and published in January 1776, which proclaimed the necessity of independence and democracy. This 25,000-word pamphlet spoke to the man in the street, basing the arguments for independence on both moral and practical grounds. Paine maintained that continued union with Great Britain was both unrealistic and undesirable.

> 'Tis repugnant to reason, to the universal order of things, to all examples from former ages, to suppose that this continent can long remain subject to any external power. The most sanguine in Britain doth not think it so. The utmost stretch of human wisdom cannot, at this time, compass a plan, short of separation, which can promise the continent even a year's security. Reconciliation is now a fallacious dream. Nature has deserted the connection, and art cannot supply her place.

This was the political environment on June 7, when Lee, a Virginia delegate to the Congress, presented a resolution proposing that Congress "declare the United Colonies free and independent states.

Three days later, Jefferson was appointed to a five-man committee that was charged with the

Revolutionary war

British soldiers in a Revolutionary War reenactment

task of preparing a formal announcement of independence. The goal was to both enlist foreign support for the American Revolution and to increase enthusiasm for the fight at home.

Jefferson was the youngest on the committee (he was only thirty-three years old), which included the well-known statesmen John Adams and Benjamin Franklin, but he was highly regarded for his writing skills. He was also a member of the delegation from Virginia, which was the colony with the largest population. Jefferson was the one who did the actual writing of the Declaration, although the committee certainly contributed suggestions after Jefferson submitted his draft.

In writing the Declaration of Independence, Jefferson pulled upon numerous sources that were widely read at the time. The English political philosopher John Locke had a great impact on the Declaration of Independence. Locke's

Natural Rights

Natural rights are those rights that are necessary for human beings to fulfill their potential. These rights are "natural" because they are based on the nature of human beings and the nature of existence itself. Natural rights are, in other words, the conditions that are necessary for a nation of people to realize their birthright—that which they deserve simply because they are human.

Thomas Jefferson

"Second Treatis of Government," written in 1690, was an attempt to justify the English revolution of 1688. In Locke's words, the work was written "to justify to the world the people of England, whose love of their just and natural rights, with their resolution to preserve them, saved the nation when it was on the very brink of slavery and ruin."

As in the Declaration of Independence, Locke begins his work with a statement of "natural" laws, which hold that no one should harm another's life, health, liberty, or possessions. For Locke, however, a ***social compact*** is necessary, under which indi-

*A **social compact** is the unwritten, voluntary agreement between members of a society to act in a responsible way and accept the authority of the state, which in turn upholds certain moral principles; its philosophy strongly favors more social equality for all parts of society.*

"We hold these truths to be self-evident, that all men are created equal; that they are endowed by their Creator with certain inalienable rights; that among these are life, liberty, and the pursuit of happiness."
—The Declaration of Independence

viduals give to the community the right of enforcing the law of reason. But while the right to enforce the law is given up, the individuals retain their natural rights. Under such an arrangement, the government established by the people is the supreme power, but it cannot be ***arbitrary***. It can hold only the powers that are given to it by law.

An essential part of Locke's theory of government is that the power of the people exceeds the government's. Under extreme conditions, he maintains, the government could be dissolved. "There remains still in the people a supreme power to remove or alter the Legislative, when they find the Legislative act contrary to the Trust reposed in them," he wrote.

One important difference between the natural rights stated by the Declaration of Independence and those claimed by Locke is that Jefferson leaves out the "right" to own property in the Declaration of Independence. Various explanations have been given for this. Some have pointed out that at a time when the majority of the population did not, in fact, own property such a right could scarcely have been politically realistic. Others have seen the omission as more fundamental to Jefferson's political philosophy. People have the "right" to the pursuit of happiness, which may involve owning property, but is not the right to own property in and of itself. Jefferson distrusted inherited fortunes, and he did not want to enshrine the right to property in the Declaration.

THE CONTENT OF THE DECLARATION OF INDEPENDENCE

The Declaration of Independence itself has four distinct parts. The ***preamble*** explains the purpose of the document. The second paragraph

Rough draft of the Declaration of Independence

Why didn't Jefferson trust inherited fortunes?

In England, society was traditionally based around several class levels. A person's class usually depended on whether or not he had inherited land from his family. Upper-class men had land passed on to them from previous generations (women could not inherit land), and these men were considered to be "better" than the lower classes. Jefferson did not agree. He did not believe that possessing property should entitle a person to special treatment.

sets out the philosophy of government based on the natural rights of people. In the middle, is a long list of charges against King George III, aiming to prove that he was a ***tyrant*** who didn't deserve to be obeyed. The last paragraph contains the actual Declara-tion of Independence.

While modern Americans may be most familiar with the opening and closing phrases, the members of Congress probably had the opposite set of priorities. The actual Declaration, contained in the last paragraph, surely was key for them. After this, the list of charges against King George III was next in importance, because this justified the rebellion. In the words of the Declaration, "a prince whose character is

***Arbitrary** means unlimited or unrestrained in the exercise of power.*

*A **preamble** is the introductory statement of a constitution or statute, usually stating the reasons for and intent of the law.*

*A **tyrant** is a harsh ruler with absolute power.*

The original Declaration of Independence has faded with age.

thus marked by every act which may define a tyrant."

The charges against the king can also be viewed as a list of American political commitments. For example, the first six charges concern the ***legislature*** and ***legislative process***, understandable considering the importance ascribed by the Americans to local government. The seventh charge concerns immigration, and can be seen as a commitment to westward expansion. Charges eight and nine concern the king's interference with the ***judicial process***, and the asserted preference for a judicial process free from ***executive interference***. Indeed, the list of charges can also be read as a ***bill*** of rights. The list of charges indirectly defines and describes the rights of a people, providing a sense of basic values and commitments.

The Declaration also implies that there are four conditions that any government must fulfill if it is going to guarantee equal rights to life, liberty, and the pursuit of happiness. It must pass laws necessary for the public good. No group should be denied adequate representation of its ***collective interest***. Justice must be administered fairly. And people should not be

murdered or otherwise harmed by their government.

Also, through the entire list, a commitment to two orders of government is made, with most of the charges concerning the king stemming from his actions against one or several of the states, rather than against all the states. This suggests a commitment to protect state government, which hints at some aspects of the U.S. Constitution. (We'll discuss that more in chapter 2.)

*The **legislature** is a body of persons with the power to create law.*

***Legislative process** is the continuing activities necessary in creating law, collecting taxes, and setting aside finances for specific uses.*

***Judicial process** is the steps taken in trying all legal cases.*

***Executive interference** means an authority exceeds its limits.*

*A **bill** is the draft of a law presented to a legislature for enactment; also, the law itself.*

***Collective interest** means the shared concerns of a group.*

THE IMPLICATIONS OF THE DECLARATION OF INDEPENDENCE

One significant change was made in the draft of the Declaration of Independence submitted by Jefferson before Congress approved the final document. Jefferson originally included a long charge regarding the King's role in the slave trade of the colonies, but this was removed in the final version. Various reasons have been given for this. According to Jefferson, the section was removed in order to please the colonies South Carolina and Georgia, "who never attempted to restrain the importation of slaves, and who on the contrary still wished to continue it." In the years to come, some Southern politicians would deny that the Declaration of

Independence was even signed by representatives from their colonies. These southerners were uncomfortable with the Declaration's strong ***affirmation*** of the rights of Americans to "life, liberty and the pursuit of happiness." The practice of slavery did not fit well with the philosophy behind the Declaration.

The reputation of the document and its author have varied over the years. While Americans celebrated the Fourth of July in the immediate years after independence, they did not pay much attention to the Declaration of Independence, and less attention to its writer. In fact, while the original Northern states incorporated the "free and equal" wording into the preambles of their constitutions, the Southern states made some changes. In the founding documents of Alabama, Arkansas, Florida, Kentucky, Mississippi and Texas, the wording was changed to "all

Lincoln Memorial

freemen, when they form a social compact, are equal."

Probably the most powerful tribute to Jefferson's work came "four score and seven years" after the signing of the Declaration of Independence. When President Abraham Lincoln made his Gettysburg Address on November 19, 1863, on a bloody Civil War battlefield, he referred explicitly to the notion that not only a new political identity had been formed, but this nation was founded on a new concept: That all men are created equal.

This is the central concept at the heart of the Declaration of Independence. This idea is still a major key to understanding what makes America the country it is today.

Affirmation *means confirmation, validation—an indication of support.*

Independence Hall in Philadelphia where the Declaration of Independence was written

LIBERTY
THE CONSTITUTION

Two
THE CONSTITUTION

Ever since the United States became a nation, the Constitution has stood at the center of American law. The judicial system determines if American practices and laws are legitimate by holding them up to the Constitution's standards. Anything determined to be "unconstitutional" is, by definition, illegal in the United States of America. Although the Constitution has been amended (or changed) over the years, its basic principles remain the same.

THE BIRTH OF THE CONSTITUTION

Before the discussions about what would become the U.S. Constitution even started in May 1787, the workmen began nailing shut the windows of the Old State House in Philadelphia. Despite the hot and humid summer that everyone knew lay ahead, the drastic step of sealing the building was taken to ensure that the public wouldn't know what the delegates to the Constitutional Convention discussed. The members of the convention feared that if people on the street were to judge the various proposals too soon, debate on the issues would be hindered. The delegates wanted to be able to consider all proposals, and change their minds and votes without concern about public opinion or political concerns.

In fact, the environment surrounding the special convention was filled with political dan-

Old State House

Capricious *means impulsive, unpredictable; inconstant.*

An ***arsenal*** *is a place that stores or manufactures arms and military equipment.*

gers. As George Washington, who had agreed to attend the convention, put it in a letter to American statesman John Jay one year before the convention:

> Things cannot go on in the same train for ever. It is much to be feared, as you observe, that the better kind of people, being disgusted with the circumstances, will have their minds prepared for any revolution whatever. We are apt to run from one extreme into another.

The problem was that the United States had been governed by the Articles of Confederation since 1781. This document established a weak Congress with few powers. It couldn't raise money. It couldn't regulate commerce between the states. And no law could be passed by it without the unanimous vote of all thirteen states. If a law were passed, the national Congress had no power to enforce it. Into the vacuum of power, state legislatures had taken on judiciary and executive roles. In other words, the state lawmakers were acting like judges and little "Presidents." Their ***capricious*** actions caused resentment among many Americans. While a peace treaty with Great Britain had been signed, some state legislatures failed to recognize some of its aspects, continuing to persecute Tories who had opposed the American Revolution.

One overwhelming issue was the war debt of $42 million. Congress couldn't force the states to pay. In 1786, Daniel Shays led a rebellion of farmers in western Massachusetts who were hard hit by the state's efforts to collect the debt. The rebels attacked a national ***arsenal*** and called for the issuance of paper money to ease

their debts. Massachusetts was in a virtual state of war, and leaders in other states feared that the rebellion could spread. On February 21, 1786, the Confederation Congress approved the calling of the special convention to change the Articles of Confederation. In fact, the articles were entirely replaced by the new U.S. Constitution.

On May 25, 1787, the delegates to the convention began to consider how to change the government. The fundamental problem was how to ensure that the government, which would rule the people, could itself be controlled. If the states needed to be united by a national government, how would that government be directed?

Fortunately, the delegates to the convention approached the task in an optimistic and experimental spirit. Many also had participated in the drafting of their own states' constitutions. Five principles guided their approach to designing a new blueprint for the United States government.

1. FEDERALISM

The Articles of Confederation had given too much power to states. The remedy was to create a new "national" government, which would control the activities of the state governments. Each level of government would be granted separate powers.

2. SEPARATION OF POWERS

Separate judiciary, executive, and legislative branches were created, each with different powers. This principle would ensure that no one group of people would be able to impose its will on the whole government. Each branch would have clearly defined different responsibilities.

3. CHECKS AND BALANCES

Each one of these separate branches would have the ability to check the actions of another. The President, for example, could appoint judges, but the judges would be able to decide questions of legality. The President could veto the laws of Congress, but Congress could also remove the President from office.

Signing the Constitution

4. MAJORITY RULE

The government would be responsive to the people, because it would be elected in frequent elections. Laws would be enacted and legal cases decided by majority vote.

5. UNALIENABLE RIGHTS

The majority would rule, but the rights of the minorities should be protected by the Constitution.

6. THE CONSTITUTION'S ORIGINAL PRINCIPLES

These principles may be seen in the Constitution today, but they were not clearly spelled out from the start. Only the outline of the final document could be glimpsed at the start.

On May 29, Edmund Randolph presented the Virginia Plan, which was to serve as a starting point for discussion. The fifteen resolutions of the plan called for a two-house legislature with representation proportional to the population of the member states, a national executive, and a national judiciary. The lower house was to be elected by American voters, but the upper house, the executive branch, and the judiciary would be appointed by the lower house. While under the Articles of Confederation all changes had to be approved by state legislatures, the plan put forward by Randolph went around the state governments, seeking a special convention from each state to ***ratify*** the new plan. From the very start, it was clear that the new plan completely put aside the principle of ***confederation***. After the convention gave preliminary approval for the Virginia Plan, it voted to establish a "national" government, with its own legislative, judicial, and executive branches.

Statue of Lady Justice

As it eventually was passed, the Constitution contains seven articles. The first article describes functions and selection of the national congress. The second article concerns the nation's chief executive, the President. The third article describes the functions of the federal

courts. The last four articles concern the relations between the state and federal governments.

Two large compromises were made to fashion the Constitution. For one thing, the colonies were composed of both large and small states. The small states, such as New Jersey and Delaware, feared that their interests would not be adequately represented

*To **ratify** means to formally sanction and approve; to confirm.*

***Confederation** refers to a league of allies, separate political bodies that have agreed to work together.*

in a legislature that was elected just on the basis of population. But large states like Virginia thought that if each state were just granted a fixed number of representatives, the power of small states would not be proportional to their size. The compromise was to have a U.S. Senate, composed of two senators from each state. The U.S. House of Representatives would be made up of representatives, allocated to each state on the basis of its population.

Another compromise was on the issue of slavery. The word "slavery" appears only once in the U.S.

Capitol Building, Washington, D.C.

Constitution as it exists today—when it is abolished by the 13th Amendment. In the main body of the Constitution, slaves are referred to as "other persons" or "such persons," for example. But the delegates argued vehemently on the subject, and five ***provisions*** of the Constitution deal with slaves directly.

The biggest political problem was that the Southern states had large populations, but much of the population was composed of slaves. The Southern leaders were certainly not about to free their slaves and give them the right to vote, but the support of the Southern states was vital to creating the new Constitution. After more than a month and a half of debate, the convention adopted a provision that would count each slave as three-fifths of a person, for the purpose of election to the House of Representatives. The compromise would be bitterly regretted by opponents of slavery in years to come. The great nineteenth-century ***abolitionist*** William Lloyd Garrison denounced the Constitution as a bargain struck between freedom and slavery. The states were united by a "***covenant*** with death" and "an agreement with Hell," he said.

The provision to abolish slavery, of course, eventually did become incorporated into the U.S. Constitution. One of the Constitution's greatest strengths, in fact, is its flexibility. At 4,400 words, it is the shortest and oldest written constitution of any government in

William Lloyd Garrison

Provisions *are measures taken to provide or stipulate certain legal actions.*

An ***abolitionist*** *was someone who wanted to bring an end to slavery.*

A ***covenant*** *is a promise, pledge, or contract.*

the world. The fact that it is so brief means that it does not spell out every possible circumstance that Americans may encounter—and this in turn means that the courts must periodically review laws to ensure that they are constitutional.

CHANGING THE CONSTITUTION

The writers of the U.S. Constitution also provided for ***amendments*** to the document, but they did not make it easy to change the U.S. Constitution. They did not think that the nation's law should be changed casually. Article Five of the Constitution provides that either the U.S. Congress or the states can propose amendments. If two-thirds of each house of Congress approve an amendment, it is sent to the states. When a majority vote of the legislatures in three-quarters of the states ratifies the amendment, it goes into effect. Also, if two-thirds of the states petition Congress, it must call a national convention to consider the amendment—but this has not yet happened.

Over the years, about a thousand amendments to the constitution have been proposed; only twenty-seven of those have been adopted. Some of the more important amendments have:

- provided for the direct election of senators
- given women the vote
- lowered the voting age to eighteen
- allowed for a national income tax to be imposed

Women protestors demanded the right to vote

Andrew Jackson

The 18th Amendment prohibited alcohol production and sales, while the 21st Amendment ***repealed*** Prohibition.

The Constitution does allow great flexibility in ways far short of amendment in all three branches of government.

Suffragists picketing the White House, 1917.

Putting the Constitution into Practice

The Supreme Court, the highest level of the judicial branch, has the ultimate authority for interpretation of the Constitution. It depends on the other branches of government, however, for enforcement of its rulings. For example, in 1832, when the Supreme Court ruled that a federal treaty with the Cherokee Indians in Georgia was binding, President Andrew Jackson simply refused to honor its judgment. In the end, the U.S. Army forced the Cherokee out of Georgia.

Congress, the legislative branch, is granted "all ***inherent*** powers" to fulfill its role. This means, for example, it can establish commissions to inform itself on various issues, but it does not mean that it can start investigations purely to expose people to public criticism or possible later prosecution. It also cannot delegate legislative power to private groups or give up its authority to government agencies. During the Great Depression, for example, the Supreme Court ruled that parts of the National Recovery Act were unconsti-

Amendments *are things added on, usually in order to change a constitution or law.*

Repealed *means taken back or annulled by authoritative act.*

Inherent *has to do with the essential nature of something.*

tutional because the Congress had given away too much of its power to legislate. Congress can, however, establish independent agencies such as the Federal Trade Commission, and the power of these independent bodies has grown tremendously in recent decades.

The executive power resides in the President of the United States, but this has meant different things over time too. There have been periods in this country, such as in the last decades of the 1800s, when the legislative branch has assumed greater importance than the presidency. Beginning with the first presidencies of the last century, however, the role of the President has grown to its dominant position. President Theodore Roosevelt referred to the presidency as a "bully pulpit," but he also took concrete actions to establish greater presidential control over the federal government.

Today, the President proposes the annual budget, which then must be approved by the House of Representatives. The President also

Bombing in Korea

has responsibility for conducting foreign affairs, negotiating treaties and naming ***ambassadors***. According to the Constitution, Congress must formally approve a declaration of war. In fact, this has not occurred since World War II, yet Presidents have committed military forces in action from the Korean Conflict in 1950 to the invasion of Iraq in 2003 with no formal declaration of war.

Although the Constitution has been amended twenty-seven times, it remains the primary document that shapes American law and thinking. Without the Constitution, the United States would be a very different nation.

***Ambassadors** are official people chosen to represent one government in its dealings with another.*

Anti-Vietnam War demonstration

Congress OF THE United

begun and held at the City of New-York, on

Wednesday the fourth of March, one thousand seven hundre

THE Conventions of a number of the States, having at the time of their adopting

declaratory and restrictive clauses should be added: And as extending the ground of public confidence in

RESOLVED by the Senate and House of Representatives of the United

ticles be proposed to the Legislatures of the several States, as amendments to the Constitution of the United

all intents and purposes, as part of the said Constitution; viz.

ARTICLES in addition to, and Amendment of the Constitution of the Unite

to the fifth Article of the original Constitution.

umeration required by the first Article of the Constitution, there shall be one Representative for every thirt

ation shall be so regulated by Congress, that there shall be not less than one hundred Representa

ber of Representatives shall amount to two hundred, after which the proportion shall be so regulated by

ne Representative for every fifty thousand persons.

U.S. Bill of Rights

g the compensation for the services of the Senators and Representatives, shall take effect, until an election

Three
THE BILL OF RIGHTS

The City of San Francisco sues the State of California to allow same-sex marriage. In its suit, the city contends that the state's family code violates the Constitution's equal protection clause and its due process clause by not giving equal opportunity to same-sex couples.

Two policemen arrest a suspect, and as the handcuffs are being put on, one of the police begins to recite the "Miranda" rights—"You have the right to an attorney. . ."—a list of rights familiar to anyone who has watched TV police dramas.

Powerful lobbyists in Washington complain about the new campaign finance law. The new regulations, they say, abridge their rights under the 1st Amendment.

These three scenes involve quite different principles, but all concern one document that is fundamental to the freedoms that Americans sometimes take for granted: the Bill of Rights. This list of the first ten amendments to the U.S. Constitution is often referred to but little read. These amendments were critical to obtaining the acceptance of the U.S. Constitution two centuries ago, and continue to be vital to protecting the rights of Americans today.

The Bill of Rights guarantees that a person accused of a crime still has basic rights.

The first ten amendments to the U.S. Constitution guarantee these rights (among others):

- the free exercise of religion
- freedom of the press
- freedom of speech
- freedom of assembly (in other words, people cannot be kept from meeting together)
- the right to a trial by jury
- the right to bear arms
- the right to a speedy trial
- protection from seizure (when property is taken by the police or other government representatives) and search without a warrant
- the right to due process (the various procedures involved with a fair trial)
- protection from cruel and unusual punishment

As in the case of the Constitution, the Bill of Rights was preceded by previous similar documents. We can see its roots extending all the way back to the Magna Carta, the document composed in 1215 that established the principle that even the King of England had to answer to the law. More immediate precedents can easily be found in the governments of American colonies. Eight states already had adopted bills of rights before the U.S. Constitution was written.

__Redundant__ means more than what is necessary or normal.

Nonetheless, the U.S. Constitution at first didn't include any Bill of Rights. It was not considered by some of the main writers of the Constitution to be necessary. First, many people considered that the problem facing the new nation at that point was too much liberty, rather than too much authority. Second, some of the writers of the Constitution thought that the rights now guaranteed by the first ten amendments to the Constitution should be understood to be already granted by the Constitution. To guarantee the rights, they said, would just be ***redundant***.

Freedom of religion

When the first elected Congress got down to business in 1789, one of the first items on the agenda was to pass a national Bill of Rights. James Madison, who is sometimes deemed the "Father of the Constitution" because of his work on the founding document, originally argued that a Bill of Rights was not needed. But before the first session of Congress, he read through the various state's bills of rights, and produced roughly twenty amendments. Of these, twelve ended up being passed by the Senate and House. These were sent to the state legislatures, which approved all but two. The remaining ten were ratified by the necessary number of states and now constitute our Bill of Rights.

The Bill of Rights was originally intended to keep the federal government from interfering with the basic rights of citizens. An amendment that would have also restricted the powers of state governments was defeated during debate in the Senate. The Supreme Court in 1833 ruled that, in fact, the Bill of Rights didn't apply to the states. But the 14th Amendment, ratified in 1868, says in part: "nor shall any State deprive any person of life, liberty or property without due process of law." In recent years, this clause has been used to ensure that the Bill of Rights is observed by state governments too.

U.S. justice system

The protections offered by the Bill of Rights have been interpreted differently over the years. The Supreme Court makes the ultimate decision about when a government policy contradicts the Bill of Rights, but its interpretations of the laws have varied widely. One Supreme Court verdict may be contradicted by a subsequent decision years later, as the Court's legal philosophy changes with the times.

The judicial power to protect rights also has certain limitations. First of all, somebody must bring the issue to court. In order to bring a legal suit, however, the ***plaintiff*** must have "standing." This means that the party

*A **plaintiff** is someone who brings a legal action.*

The Bill of Rights protects freedom of the press

bringing the suit can show that he or she suffered an injury recognized by the law. An individual can't bring a matter to court for an injury suffered by someone else.

Courts also presume that official acts have some validity. This means that the plaintiff not only has to prove his or her point; the argument must also have extra weight to tip the balance against the government's position.

Even if a court decides that a case involving civil rights has merit and rules for a plaintiff, that judgment won't necessarily apply to similar cases. Technically, the decision binds only the parties to the suit. If a case involves a constitutional question, however, and is decided by the Supreme Court, its application will be much broader.

Perhaps as important as the court decisions is the guidance that the Bill of Rights gives to both lawmakers and the general public. The freedoms of religion and speech, for example, are so basic that many Americans don't even realize that these are legal guarantees, not just cultural traditions. But when efforts to restrict these rights are made, Americans have not been shy about resorting to the courts to make sure that their rights are observed.

Text of the Bill of Rights

The First Amendment
Congress shall make no law respecting an establishment of religion or prohibiting the free exercise thereof; or abridging the freedom of speech, or of the press; of the right of the people peaceably to assemble and to petition the Government for a redress of grievances.

The Second Amendment
A well-regulated Militia, being necessary to the security of a free State, the right of the people to keep and bear Arms, shall not be infringed.

The Third Amendment
No Soldier shall, in time of peace be quartered in any house, without the consent of the Owner, nor in time of war, but in a manner to be prescribed by law.

The Fourth Amendment
The right of the people to be secure in their persons, houses, papers and effects, against unreasonable searches and seizures, shall not be violated, and no Warrants shall issue, but upon probable cause, supported by oath or affirmation, and particularly describing the place to be searched, and the persons or things to be seized.

The Fifth Amendment
No person shall be held to answer for a capital, or otherwise infamous crime, unless on a presentment or indictment of a Grand Jury, except in cases arising in the land or naval forces, or in the Militia, when in actual service in time of war or public danger; nor shall any person be subject for the same offense to be twice put in jeopardy of life or limb; nor shall be compelled in any criminal case to be a witness against himself; nor be deprived of life, liberty, or property, without due process of law; nor shall private property be taken for public use, without just compensation.

The Sixth Amendment
In all criminal prosecutions, the accused shall enjoy the right to a speedy and public trial, by an impartial jury of the State and district wherein the crime shall have been committed, which district shall have been previously ascertained by law, and to be informed of the nature and cause of the accusation; to be confronted with the witnesses against him; to have compulsory process for obtaining witnesses in his favor; and to have the Assistance of Counsel for his defense.

The Seventh Amendment
In suits at common law, where the value in controversy shall exceed twenty dollars, the right of trial by jury shall be preserved, and no fact tried by a jury, shall be otherwise reexamined in any Court of the United States, than according to the rules of common law.

The Eighth Amendment
Excessive bail shall not be required nor excessive fines imposed, nor cruel and unusual punishments inflicted.

The Ninth Amendment
The enumeration in the Constitution of certain rights, shall not be construed to deny or disparage others retained by the people.

The Tenth Amendment
The powers not delegated to the United States by the Constitution, nor prohibited by it to the States, are reserved to the States respectively, or to the people.

Vote
Here

E-90

Four
THE ELECTORAL COLLEGE

A common nightmare scenario is imagined every four years: a U.S. President is put in office after an election where the "wrong winner wins." The election in 2000 was no exception. This time the winner of the presidency "again" did not win the popular vote of the American people.

Again?

Yes, George W. Bush won 277 electoral votes, but he received 500,000 fewer actual votes from the people than the Democratic Party nominee, Al Gore, who received 266 electoral votes and lost the election. The 2000 vote was historic in that it was the first time the U.S. Supreme Court intervened in an election, suspending a recount of votes, but the election of 2000 was far from the first time that the victor didn't win the popular vote. This scenario, in fact, goes back to the virtual origin of the Electoral College. Since the founding of the country, seventeen elections have been held in which no candidate received a popular vote majority. Aside from the election of 2000, the races of 1876, 1888, and probably 1960 were cases when the winner of the popular vote didn't win a majority of votes in the Electoral College.

While the selection of a President is obviously important, the process didn't get as much attention as some other parts of the Constitution when the founding document was being written. For one thing, most of the people involved in the drafting of the Constitution already assumed the first President was going to be George Washington. In fact, in the first election, he did receive a unanimous vote from the appointed electors. After his election, some of the Founding Fathers thought the Congress would assume a primary role in selecting the President.

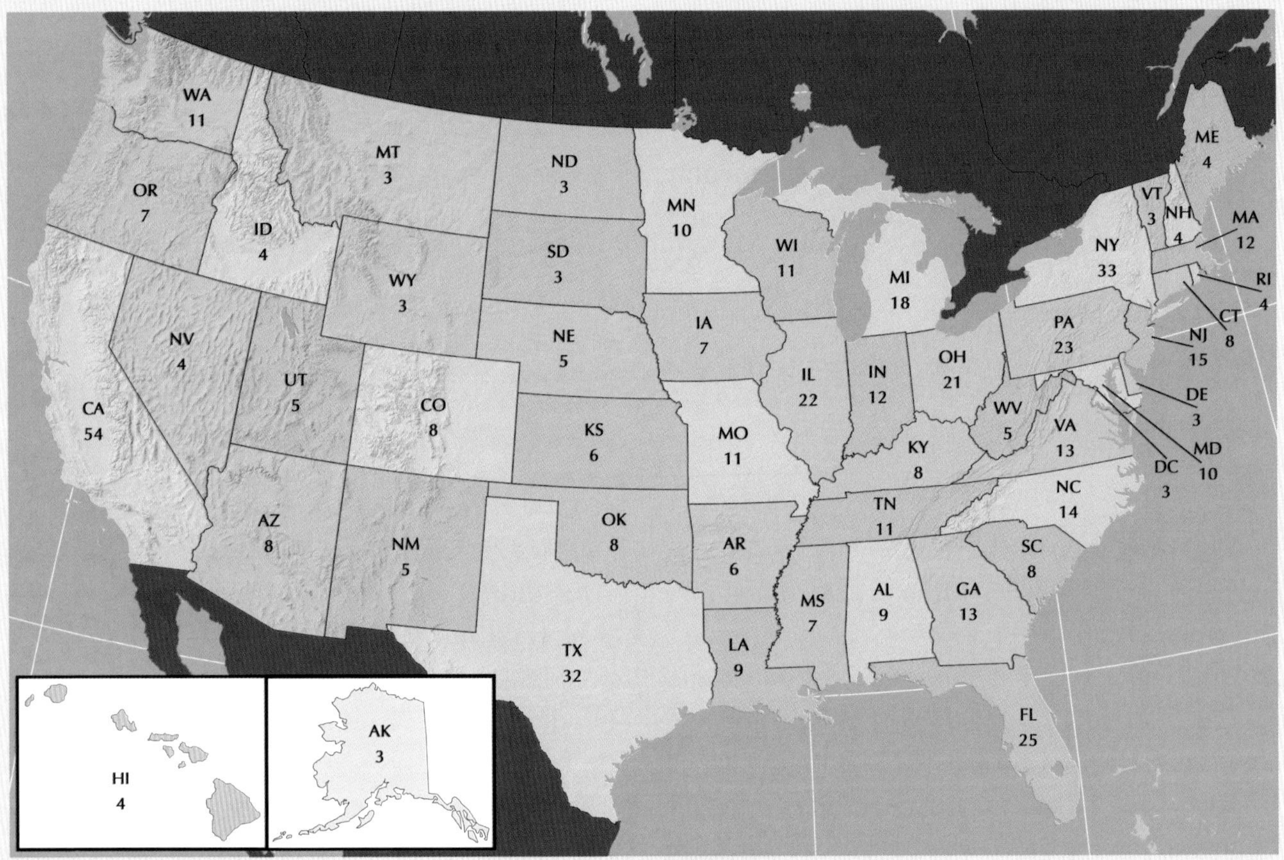

Electoral map showing the number of votes each state has in the Electoral College

Originally, the Constitution called for an executive branch that would be dependent on the legislature. Not until two weeks before the Constitutional Convention adjourned did it receive a committee proposal to elect a President and Vice President using an electoral college.

The electoral college, like many aspects of the Constitution, was created as a compromise to make both large and small states happier. The framers of the Constitution also doubted that a national leader could gather enough backing to be chosen in the new country, which had a primitive communications and transportation system.

The Founding Fathers distrusted political parties, and tried to create a government that would make the growth of political parties impossible. The Electoral College, as originally ***conceived***, would be composed of politically independent and distinguished citizens chosen by state legislators. The number of each state's electors would equal its representation in the U.S. House and Senate. Ironically, the framers who created a Constitution that sought to decrease the influence of political parties actually created a system where political parties were necessary in order to make the presidential selection process function.

During the Washington administration (1789–1793), the Federalist Party began to form, along with the opposition Democratic-Republican Party. The Democratic-Republicans, who gathered around Thomas Jefferson, championed limited national government. They opposed the Federalists, whose ideas encouraged a government controlled by a special elite ***aristocracy***.

By the 1800 election, however, the party system was fully established and electors were a group of men chosen by each party, pledged to vote for their party's candidate.

The flaws in the system became clear in that election. According to the procedure outlined in Article 2 of the Constitution, the electors of 1800 cast two votes each, without saying who was for Vice President or President. The person with the highest number of votes was to be President. The Democratic party had a majority of members in the electoral college, but the election was tied between Thomas Jefferson and Aaron Burr.

George Washington

An aristocracy *is government by a small privileged class.*

Conceived *means thought out at the beginning; mentally created.*

Eventually, the House of Representatives chose Thomas Jefferson, but the final selection was bitter and surrounded by controversy. The House required thirty-six ballots before Jefferson was declared the winner with ten votes.

The 1800 presidential vote and its ***repercussions*** led directly to the 12th Amendment to the Constitution, which was ratified in 1804. This amendment requires electors to specify which candidate is for Vice President and which is for President. The winner of the race must receive 270 out of 538 votes of the Electoral College.

The race could still be thrown into the House of Representatives, however, if no person received more than 270 votes. After the 12th Amendment was passed, the only

Repercussions *are the indirect effects, influences, or results that are produced by an event or action.*

Voting booth

Aaron Burr

John Quincy Adams

time this happened was in 1824, when the two-party system broke down and four candidates were nominated. John Quincy Adams, the son of the first Federalist President, was elected, even though he received fewer electoral votes than Andrew Jackson.

The 12th Amendment fixed one flaw, and it indirectly fostered the current two-party system that dominates the United States political system. The need to establish a national majority in the Electoral College vote means that third parties can seldom win, even though they can sometimes win most of the votes in a few states. Since the Civil War, only five third-party candidates have won electoral votes. In 1992, for example, Ross Perot was a well-funded candidate with a strong base of support. He won nearly 19 percent of the nationwide presidential vote, the strongest third-party showing since 1912. But he did not receive any electoral votes.

The requirement that a candidate must win most of the votes in order to win an individual state, along with the requirement for a majority in the Electoral College to win the presidency, makes third-party candidacies difficult. The best they can do is play a "spoiler" role by preventing either of the two major parties from winning an Electoral College majority. If such a

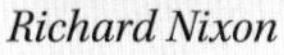

Richard Nixon

Hubert Humphrey

deadlock were ever thrown into the House of Representatives for the selection of a President, it's extremely unlikely that the members of the dominant two parties would choose a third-party candidate as the President. At best, the hope for third-party candidates is that their ideas will be adopted by the major parties.

Another factor that affects the political landscape in America at all levels is the dominant role of the "single district plurality" system. This means simply that a voter casts a single vote for each official to be elected, and the candidate receiving the most votes wins the position. Even when there are more than two serious candidates and a majority of votes is difficult to get, a plurality is sufficient to be elected in most of America. The only exception to this rule in federal general elections are in the District of Columbia and Georgia, which require that a candidate receive a majority of popular votes in order to be elected. Georgia requires a run-off election for state elected officials under the same circumstances, and in Vermont state officials are elected by the state legislature when no majority is obtained in the general election.

One natural consequence of this system is that two parties dominate the federal, state, and local levels. But these two parties need not always be the same ones. The current rivalry between the Republicans and Democrats is more than 140 years old, but it is the third two-party rivalry in this country.

The incentives created by the Electoral College rules also mean that American voters think strategically so they don't "waste" their votes on third-party candidates. Polls regularly show that many voters are unwilling to vote for a third-party candidate, even if that candidate has preferable positions on the issues.

The Republican and Democratic parties

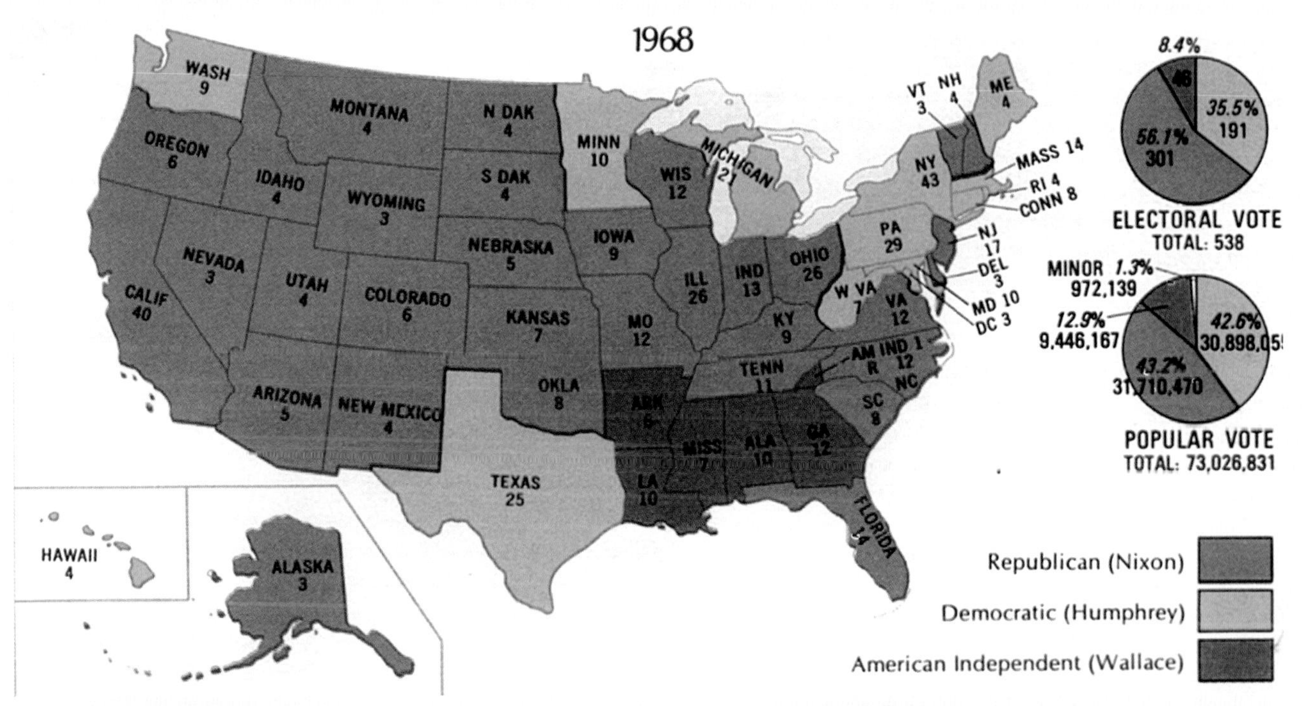

Map of presidential election, 1968.

know how voters think, and they often convey messages about the bad consequences if their candidates lose. For example, in the 1968 election, when Republican candidate Richard Nixon ran against Democrat Hubert Humphrey, the Republicans had to worry about the third-party candidacy of George Wallace. Understandably, the Nixon campaign rolled out the slogan "A Vote for Wallace is a vote for Humphrey."

The Electoral College strengthens the two-party system in other ways. Because the two parties are fighting for control at the federal level, the parties' structure resembles the government's structure, with similar delegation of responsibilities. Also, because the Electoral College gives such importance to the total state vote, party organization at the state level is also very important. In turn, the state level of government is given special importance because of the significance of the state party.

Backers of the Electoral College system maintain that it creates a relatively low-conflict

and practical system. Other political systems, they say, create more bitter ***ideological*** battles. The Electoral College encourages political movements to try to influence the dominant parties from within, rather than trying to capture the presidency with their own third party. Over time, it's within the interest of both Republicans and Democrats to include issues that are seized upon by third parties. As the two ***dominant*** parties try to bring in as many political interests as possible, their positions often change to become like that of the majority.

Ideological *means concerned with or relating to ideas.*

Dominant *means stronger.*

The Donkey and the Elephant

Why do a donkey and an elephant represent today's political parties?

The donkey was first associated with Democrat Andrew Jackson's 1828 presidential campaign. His opponents called him a jackass (a donkey), and Jackson decided to use the image of the strong-willed animal on his campaign posters. Later, cartoonist Thomas Nast used the Democratic donkey in newspaper cartoons and made the symbol famous.

Nast invented another famous symbol—the Republican elephant. After the Republicans did badly in the election of 1874, Nast drew a cartoon of an elephant in a trap. He chose the elephant to represent people who had voted Republican because elephants are strong but easily frightened.

Other cartoonists picked up the symbols and used them in their drawings, until each party became connected with its own animal. Today, Democrats say the donkey is smart and brave, while Republicans say the elephant is strong and dignified.

Although it has changed substantially over the years, the Democratic Party now claims to be the oldest organized political party in the world.

Martin Luther King, Jr.

Five
ENDING THE LEGACY OF SLAVERY

The spring of 1963 was brutal in Birmingham, Alabama. While the followers of Martin Luther King Jr. sought nonviolent means to desegregate lunch counters and other public accommodations, they were met with force from the city's police commissioner, Eugene "Bull" Connor. Across the nation, newspapers carried the photos from the confrontations, pictures of school children and other peaceful marchers bitten by police attack dogs and forced back with fire hoses. More than a hundred years after the army of the Confederacy had surrendered at Appomatox, it seemed like the Civil War was still being fought.

In fact, the nonviolent resistance achieved some of its goals. The events of 1963 did prompt passage of the landmark Civil Rights Act of 1964, but to better understand its origins and the problem of race in America, we have to go back more than a century.

When the U.S. Constitution was written, slavery was protected by several clauses. Despite efforts to limit the institution, the critical constitutional amendments to end slavery were not approved until after the Civil War.

The 13th Amendment, which became effective in 1865, abolished slavery or involuntary servitude. The amendment also made slavery a federal crime, the first time that an amendment increased the powers of Congress.

The 14th Amendment made it clear that all people born or naturalized in the United States are citizens of the United States. Prior to the Civil War, African Americans born in the United

Lyndon Johnson signing Civil Rights Act

States couldn't become American citizens, even if they were free and descended from people living in the original thirteen states when the Constitution was ratified. Before this amendment, a person was primarily a citizen of a state, and only secondarily a citizen of the United States. This amendment reversed the situation.

The 14th Amendment also proclaims that no state can "deprive any person of life, liberty or property without due process of law." The amendment was followed by the Civil Rights Act of 1875, which made it illegal for any person to refuse accommodations or service on the basis of race. But opponents to integration said the 14th Amendment didn't apply to actions taken by private citizens, so Congress couldn't make discrimination by private citizens illegal.

Elements of the 1875 Civil Rights Act had been debated since Senator Charles Sumner of Massachusetts introduced a national civil rights bill in 1867. The legislation had been fought bitterly by Southern Democrats, who never voted for any civil rights or voting rights bill during the entire nineteenth century. The impact of the 1875 legislation was undercut by numerous court decisions.

For example, in the 1896 Supreme Court case of *Plessy vs. Ferguson*, an African American man was arrested for violating a law that required whites and African Americans to sit in "equal but separate" railroad cars while traveling. Plessy was tossed off the train and arrested after he insisted on sitting in the "whites only" section. The Supreme Court upheld the law under which he was arrested, saying the races could be separated as long as they were equally treated. This view, however, was not unanimous on the Court. As Judge Harlan said in his dissent:

> Our Constitution is color blind, and neither knows nor tolerates classes among citizens. The destinies of the two races in this country are indissolubly linked together, and the interests of both require that the common government of all shall not permit the seeds of race hate to be planted under the sanction of law.

Civil rights demonstrator

The substance of that dissent became law fifty-eight years later in the Supreme Court case of *Brown vs. Board of Education*, but from 1896 to 1954, hundreds of laws were passed throughout the South and in other states requiring that the races be separated in many activities.

The 15th Amendment was the last constitutional amendment directly resulting from the Civil War. It guaranteed that the "right of citizens of the United States to vote shall not be denied or abridged by the United States or by any State on account of race, color, or previous condition of servitude". This amendment was ratified in 1870, but that doesn't mean that it was always obeyed. For decades afterward, states and local governments enacted provisions that effectively denied whole classes of citizens the right to vote.

Texas, for example, had a White Primary Law that effectively took

away the right to vote from non-Whites, because practically whoever won the Democratic primary in Texas won the election. The Supreme Court ruled against this device in 1927, but the practice of exclusionary primaries continued under other forms until 1953, when the Supreme Court also ruled against a private exclusionary political club called the Jaybird Democratic Association.

Enfranchise ***Enfranchise** means to give the power to vote.*

In recent decades, a series of laws has been passed to ensure that the intent of the 15th Amendment is uniformly observed. Efforts to ban the poll tax which required voters to pay for the right to vote, began in the 1940s, but it wasn't always effective until 1962, when the 24th Amendment was finally ratified. This amendment flatly banned the use of poll taxes and made the law enforceable by Congress. The U.S. Congress also passed sweeping but ineffective civil rights acts to ***enfranchise*** African Americans in 1957 and 1960; but it wasn't until the Voting Rights Act of 1965 that electoral discrimination was effectively curbed. The Voting Rights Act proclaimed that "no voting qualification or

You Can't Vote If You Can't Read

Before 1970, many states had laws that required people to pass a reading test before they could vote. This meant that people who lacked education, had a reading disability, or spoke another language were barred from voting.

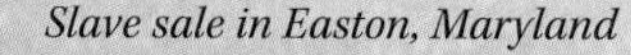
Slave sale in Easton, Maryland

prerequisite to voting" is permissible if it denies or diminishes the right to vote on account of race or color.

After the Voting Rights Act, the number of black voters grew by 11 percent in 1966 and another eight percent over the next two years. Between 1965 and 1972, the proportion of blacks registered to vote in states targeted by the act grew from 29.3 percent to 56.6 percent. These states had to take special measures to ensure that no one was discriminated against at the voting booth.

The act originally had a five-year life span, but in 1970, it was extended for another five years, and the 1970 extension revised the formula for coverage, focusing on more states and suspending literacy tests nationwide. The 1975 extension permanently banned such tests, but also

School segregation protesters

provided for voter information to be distributed in the language of local voters. In 1982, the act was extended for another 25 years.

While the bitter ***desegregation*** battles of the 1960s defeated legal segregation, America still wrestles with the question of racial discrimination. The Supreme Court recently ruled in favor of affirmative action programs aimed at improving the opportunities for minorities in higher education, but racial issues remain. African Americans now serve in the cabinet of the President of the United States, but it has been less than fifty years since legal segregation ended in this country, and its legacy endures. Much more remains to be done to ensure equal opportunities for all Americans.

Literacy *is the ability to read and write.*

Desegregation *means members of different groups are not kept separated from each other.*

U.S. currency and credit cards

Six

WHAT MAKES THE AMERICAN ECONOMY?

After the collapse of the Soviet Union in the 1990s, millions of Russians crowded around television screens for a message from America. This was not a statement about politics or human rights. It was not a broadcast from the United States encouraging Russian-American friendship. No, the message from America that obsessed so many Russians was sent via a soap opera set in sunny California: Santa Barbara. Russians were eager to catch a glimpse of what they considered to be the American lifestyle.

Forming perceptions about America from ***mass media*** images was nothing new. Previously, other countries have assumed that most Americans wore cowboy hats, like they do on *Dallas*, or that the lives of American youths are like what is depicted in *Baywatch* episodes. When people in other countries ask what defines America, their answer is not any government document or political system. Rather, it is the perception of wealth that is inconceivable to a vast majority of the world's population.

The wealth of this country does in part stem from the political system of the United States. Government policies from the very start of this nation have encouraged ***entrepreneurship***. Some critics would say that government policies have assisted the accumu-

Mass media *includes television, newspapers, radio, and magazines.*

Entrepreneurship *is the undertakings of someone organizing, managing, and assuming the risks of a business or enterprise.*

__Tariffs__ are charges imposed by a government on imported, and in some countries exported, goods.

__Subsidies__ are grants or monetary gifts.

__Indigo__ is a blue dye that comes from plants.

lation of wealth, at the cost of the greater social good.

The Revolutionary War was caused in part by a reaction of businessmen to policies of England that affected their profits. The government of England at the time generally followed an economic policy that is often referred to as mercantilism. This policy encouraged business enterprises in order to increase the power of the government. The purpose of private business, according to this line of thinking, was to enhance the power of the state, rather than the individual. Mercantilists favored close government regulation of business to ensure that the state benefited from commerce. In the mercantilist economic analysis, exports should always exceed imports, so ***tariffs*** were favored. Mercantilists supported the cre-

Russian people often wonder about the American lifestyle

ation of colonies, which would supply raw materials and markets for products made in the mother country.

But while founding the American colonies may have fit into a mercantile system originally, the inhabitants of the New World soon began chafing at the restrictions imposed by England. Beginning in 1650, the British government passed a series of laws called the Navigation Acts, which regulated colonial business for the benefit of the mother country. The British government wanted supplies of raw materials and markets, and the net cash flow went from the colonies to England. The acts forced most trade between the colonies and the rest of the world to be done by English or colonial crews. And both exports from and imports to the colonies had to make a stop in England, a provision enacted to protect the English shipping business.

The English government also placed restrictions on manufacturing some items, such as finished iron products, and ***subsidies*** on others, such as ***indigo***.

At first, few people complained about the regulations. But after the Seven Years War with the French, the Parliament sought to raise funds from the colonies. The Sugar Act of 1764 strictly

Adam Smith

enforced a tariff on sugar, and prosecuted smugglers. The Stamp Act of 1765 forced colonists to pay new taxes, and the Tea Act of 1773 eliminated colonial middlemen who had been in the tea-importing business. All of these policies further fueled the colonies' discontent.

Even within England at the time, there were voices that objected to its mercantile policies. One of the most influential was Adam Smith, who published his *Wealth of Nations* in the same year that the Declaration of Independence was declared. Smith, whose thinking influenced American revolutionary leaders like Thomas Jefferson and Alexander Hamilton, saw that the "invisible hand" of the market, rather than government bureaucrats, would most efficiently hand out resources to the public. If the market were allowed to function freely, said Smith, it would provide for ever-increasing levels of wealth and productivity. Free trade, Smith asserted, rather than mercantilism, would benefit both colony and home country. When the Americans won their freedom from England, Smith's ideas were influential among the founders of the United States.

By the time of the American Revolution, the colonists had achieved one of the highest standards of living in the world. The population of the thirteen colonies was about 2 million whites, 500,000 African Americans and 100,000 Native Americans. And although its population was only one-third of England's, the economic output of the United States equaled 40 percent of the mother country.

After the American Revolution, private enterprise was poised to profit handsomely from the new situation. The new government was

Colonial currency

naturally more responsive to American business interests than the British Crown had been. While the Articles of Confederation had clearly been unsatisfactory for commercial interests because they did not provide the means for government to pay its bills, the new Constitution included a number of provisions helpful for business development.

Congress, for example, was granted the ability to impose import duties and raise revenues. This would allow funding for naval protection and the military muscle for westward expansion. The unified power the Constitution gave the federal government to impose tariffs could be a useful tool in making national trade policy. For example, if a country were to export a certain product here, the United States could demand certain tariff concessions in return. The Con-stitution allowed for the creation of a national currency, which in turn meant that the large internal market of the new country could be efficiently developed. To this end, states were prohibited from restricting commerce. Patent and copyright laws were authorized by the new government, which safeguarded the rights of entrepreneurs to profit from inventions. A new postal system, guaranteed by the Constitution, provided firms and individuals with a reliable communication system. As a whole, the Constitution provided an exceptional legal framework to allow the free flow of goods and

Agrarians *are members of a movement or party promoting farming interests.*

Egalitarian *means marked by a social philosophy that promotes removing inequalities among people.*

Conservative *means relating to the political philosophy based on social stability and tradition; desiring to preserve what is established.*

people over the new nation.

From the start, however, there were ideological conflicts over the direction of the new country. On one hand, Alexander Hamilton, the first Secretary of the Treasury, championed the interests of the merchant and fledgling industrial sectors. The key purpose of government, he believed, was to protect private property and provide the legal structure for the accumulation of capital.

The Constitution was vital to this goal, because the government needed to be able to pay off its debts, and Hamilton was a vocal advocate of the new Constitution. But Hamilton also championed

the creation of a Bank of the United States, which combined public and private ownership. This policy and other ideas of Hamilton were more controversial.

Opposing the Hamiltonians politically was Jefferson, who distrusted bankers to put the interests of the nation first. Jefferson argued that the policies advocated by Hamilton too often served merchants and speculators, rather than ordinary Americans. Jefferson attracted the support of ***agrarians***, other leaders who wanted to develop the interior of the country and local manufacturing.

When Jefferson was elected in 1800, his Democrat-Republican Party began a period of power consolidation, and the Federalist Party represented by Hamilton soon declined. But the political tension would live on for future generations as ***egalitarian*** and ***conservative*** forces struggled against each other, reflected in policies affecting business and labor.

The industrial, communication, transporta-

Alexander Hamilton

tion, and agricultural revolutions that transformed the American economy in the early nineteenth century were assisted by government policies, but they did not depend totally on the government for their success. For example, the federal government gave engineering and surveying assistance to the nation's first railroads. In 1850, the first federal railroad land grant turned over federal lands to be used by the new railroad companies, in effect paying for the original costs of the Illinois Central Railroad. Later, the first transcontinental railroad was completed with federal incentives and support in 1869. The states also assisted, so that overall from 1815 to 1860, about 60 percent of the total investment in transportation facilities came from government.

As important as these subsidies were, however, the guidance given by the nation's judicial branch was also essential. As the Supreme Court interpreted the nation's new Constitution, it tended to give individuals great freedom for using their business talents. Court decisions also tended to support the rights of individuals to gain, hold, and use property to earn profits.

As the economy developed in the United States, a new entity became more common: the ***corporation***. The use of the corporate form of business organization in the United States at that time was much more common than in other countries, in part because state governments ***chartered*** corporations to achieve public goals. Between 1776 and 1800, state governments incorporated about three hundred companies.

By the mid- to late 1800s, companies began granting limited liability to investors, meaning that stockholders were not held per-

Nineteenth-century railroad

*A **corporation** is a legal entity created to bring individuals together for a specified purpose, with a life separate from that of its owners or stockholders.*

***Chartered** means for a government to grant special privileges to a company or institiution.*

sonally responsible for the debts of the corporation, and could lose only their investment if the company failed. Incorporation in colonial days usually was for some civic purpose, but increasingly corporations were formed primarily to make the best use of business opportunities. The nation's first general ***incorporation*** law was passed in New York in 1811, allowing simple incorporation with no special legislative act. Over the next thirty-seven years, 304 new companies incorporated under the new law. Other states followed the lead of New York, and by 1860, every state with a manufacturing industry had passed a general incorporation law.

Despite the growth in manufacturing, the railroad companies were the biggest enterprises of the day by the middle of the 1800s. The main railroads connecting the East and the Midwest employed thousands of workers, while the largest textile mills at the time employed fewer

Andrew Carnegie

than a thousand people. The railroad companies also pioneered modern management techniques. The complexity of operations demanded ***unprecedented*** levels of coordination and specialization. The Pennsylvania Railroad became known as the "standard railroad of the world" because of its model management. From the 1850s through the 1870s, the organiza- tion was streamlined, with separate treasury, legal, and accounting departments. The duties of the corporate officers were clearly defined, and financial controls were imposed that allowed the central office executives to monitor and coordinate activities in the divisions. Policymaking began to be separated from day-to-day operations.

J. Pierpont Morgan dominated American banking

One business closely associated with the growth of the railroads was the steel industry. Andrew Carnegie was superintendent of the western division of the Pennsylvania Railroad before he resigned in 1865 to pursue business interests. Those activities would lead to his entry into the steel business in 1872. Carnegie Steel soon became the largest steel company in the world. Overall, the production of steel in the United States grew from 70,000 tons in 1870 to over 4 million tons just twenty years later, providing the building material for the nation's railroads and industrial ***infrastructure***.

Incorporation *is the process of uniting a business into a single legal body.*

Infrastructure *is made up of the transportation and communications systems within a country.*

But as the economy of the United

Model T Ford assembly

States developed, the dark side of the industrial revolution began to be evident as well. Industry provided employment for millions, but the benefits were not spread around evenly. The pioneers of industry accumulated great riches, and by the 1890s, industrial leaders were often referred to as "robber barons." The federal government made some attempts to restrain some of the worst abuses by businesses, but the enforcement of the law was uneven at best. For example, Congress enacted the Interstate Commerce Act in 1887 to stabilize railroad rates, but for years it had little real impact. The Sherman Anti-Trust Act was enacted in 1890, but five of the first ten prosecutions under the new law were against ***labor unions***, rather than corporations.

As the twentieth century began, however, new currents of thought began to be evident in the world of government policy. With the presidency of Theodore Roosevelt, the government began to use the legal tools at its disposal to break up ***monopolies*** such as Standard Oil and the Northern Securities Company, a railroad holding company. In 1914, Congress created a new regulatory agency, the Federal Trade

Commission (FTC) and passed the Clayton Act, a new antitrust law. The new legislation outlawed interlocking organization in financial firms worth over $1 million, and also outlawed the practice of contracts that prohibited suppliers from doing business with other customers.

Child laborer, Newberry, South Carolina, 1908

The banking industry also came under increasing regulation in this period. With the establishment of the Federal Reserve System, the nation's currency and monetary policy came under more systematic control by the government. Under the new law, the President appointed a Federal Reserve Board of five members. Twelve district Federal Reserve banks were established, each owned by the banks of its region. National banks were required to join the new banking system, and almost all the nation's banks soon signed up.

Also, reformers began to have some success in regulating the working conditions in American industries. While the Supreme Court ruled that Congress's attempt to outlaw the employment of children was unconstitutional, local governments began to regulate what was acceptable in America's factories. Northern industrial states passed laws in the early twentieth century, for example, that restricted the hours for female employees and forbade hiring children under the age of fourteen. The first state system of workers' compensation was created in Ohio in 1911.

Several key elements of the American economy began to de-

Labor unions *are organizations made up of employees working together to ensure fair pay and working conditions.*

Monopolies *are when a particular product or service is controlled by one person or company.*

velop in the early twentieth century apart from these more activist government policies. The automobile, for example, began to change everything from Americans' leisure pursuits to urban planning. The mass production of the automobile began with the Ford Model T, which made the car affordable for most middle class Americans. There were 2.3 million automobiles registered in the country in 1915; by 1929, the number had climbed to 23 million.

American consumers increasingly became familiar with products such as the Model T through an entirely new industry: advertising. Advertising played an important role in encouraging shoppers to spend their money, stimulating growth in the economy. By 1910, expenditures on advertising came to about four percent of the national income. The industry also promoted the growth of mass media. By 1925, advertising supplied 70 percent of the total revenues of the nation's magazines and newspapers—about $1 billion. Three years later, radio stations were taking in about $10 million annually.

Increased advertising, however, did not necessarily mean price competition. In the 1920s, the nation saw nu-

Early fruit advertising

U.S. currency

Franklin Delano Roosevelt

merous mergers occur in the business community. The one hundred largest manufacturing companies increased their share of manufacturing assets from 36 percent in 1925 to 44 percent just six years later. By 1943, 70 percent of the country's manufacturing production was produced by 100 companies. One result of this was that prices became less responsive to market forces, no longer dropping automatically when demand fell.

Demand did fall, during the Great Depression, an economic catastrophe that reshaped government social and economic policies. The Depression suddenly convinced many people that the free market system could not provide for the well-being of the country. The federal government under Republican President Herbert Hoover also seemed helpless in the face of the crisis.

Franklin Delano Roosevelt, a Democrat, was elected President in 1932, pledging a "New Deal" that would involve the government in solving the economic problem. He called for changes in the relations between government and business to promote the welfare of the population and change business behavior. In any one month between 1933 and 1940, between 10 and 20 percent of the nation's population received some sort of assistance from a New Deal program.

Some of the economic fundamentals of the country also began to change during that decade. Under the Roosevelt administration, Congress passed the National Labor Relations Act, which guaranteed workers the right to bargain with employers. Labor unions soon won key victories, such as settlement of the strike against General Motors in 1937. Overall, the administration exerted steady pressure on compa-

Dwight D. Eisenhower

*The **gross net product** is the total services and goods produced by a nation during a certain period (usually a year).*

*The **per capita gross national product** is this value divided by the number of people in the nation.*

*An **embargo** is an order by a government prohibiting commerce of certain goods or with a particular country.*

nies such as GM to sit down and negotiate with strikers. Union membership went from 6.8 percent of the workforce in 1930 to 21.9 percent at the end of the Roosevelt administration in 1945.

The administration also attempted to bring some regulation into Wall Street, which had led to the crisis that began the Depression. The Securities Act of 1933 and the Securities Exchange Act of 1934 required that all publicly owned companies submit annual reports certified by independent public accountants.

Landmark social legislation passed during this period, notably the Social Security Act of 1935. This provided for protection against personal economic catastrophes, gave public assistance to certain categories of the needy, and extended public health services to mothers and children. At the time, the measure was designed to give "some measure of protection," in Roosevelt's words, to about 30 million people.

While the New Deal allowed millions to survive the Depression, many economists believe that it was World War II that finally pulled the United States out of the economic slump. Even before the United States formally entered the war, industrial production was boosted to help America's future allies. When the war mobilization began in earnest, full employment was restored. The structure of business, however, was also changed by the war, as the government fostered the growth of a few large firms. On the other hand, labor's position was consolidated, as the government endorsed the "union shop" model that required that employees hired by a unionized business had to join the union.

After World War II, the European economies were devastated

but the American economy was soon booming. Between 1945 and 1960, the ***gross net product*** of the United States rose by 52 percent, and the ***per capita gross national product*** rose by 19 percent. Over the next decade, the per capita gross national product grew by another 29 percent. The industrial production of the United States represented about 40 percent of the world's total into the 1970s. The first computer was invented in the United States, and the country led in the development of the new computer industry, revolutionizing all aspects of the economy.

Beginning in the 1970s, however, key weaknesses in the nation's economy began to be evident. The oil ***embargo*** of 1974 revealed the dependence of the United States on imported fuel, for example. The price increases in energy contributed to economic problems for the country in subsequent decades, but the nation is as dependent as ever on fossil fuels.

The Cold War between the Soviet Union and the United States also fostered the growth in what President Dwight D. Eisenhower termed "the military-industrial complex." This sector of the economy has mushroomed over the years, representing 5.8 percent of the gross national product in 1982. With the collapse of the Soviet Union in the 1990s, the budget of the Department of Defense declined, but since September 11, 2001, defense-related spending has been growing again in relation to the national economy. The terrorist attack on the United States convinced many Americans that their nation needed a strong military.

Most of us take for granted the way we think about money. We don't realize that in the world at large, Americans have a unique outlook on spending, saving, and distributing wealth. Some groups of people resent the American financial system, while others feel it has made mistakes that harm its people and the people of the world. But whether you agree or disagree with the principles behind American wealth, the fact remains: One thing that makes America America is our lifestyle, a way of living that is firmly rooted in the American economy.

Dwight D. Eisenhower's election campaign

September 11, 2001 attacks

Seven

WHAT MAKES AMERICA AMERICA IN THE TWENTY-FIRST CENTURY?

For days after September 11, 2001, Americans saw the same horrible scene replayed on television hundreds of times: two airplanes smashing into the Twin Towers of the World Trade Center, the buildings collapsing in agonizing slow motion. There have been other catastrophes in this country before September 11, 2001, but few others seemed to divide history so terribly. This country would never be the same again.

Within twenty-four hours of the attacks on the World Trade Center and the Pentagon, President George W. Bush announced that the attacks were "more than mere acts of terror. They were acts of war." He said the nation must prepare itself for a "monumental struggle between good and evil."

The fundamental problem, of course, was that the foe of the United States in this case was shadowy. President Bush was declaring war not on a nation with established borders; he was declaring war on an ill-defined group of people.

While the U.S. intelligence services soon identified Al-Qaeda, an extremist Islamic organization, as the culprits behind the scene, punishing the culprits was difficult. After the Taliban government of Afghanistan refused to surrender Osama Bin Laden (the group's leader), the United States invaded, overthrowing the Taliban in a war lasting only about two months. Two years later, however, the country remained without a stable government, the Taliban movement continued to be a menace in the country, and Bin Laden was still at large.

One year after the attacks of September 11, President Bush issued a new National Security Strategy, which stressed the right of the United States to ***preemptively*** attack any country suspected of developing the means of attacking this country. Bush backed up this approach with increased funding for the military. He requested an additional $48 billion in military spending in January 2002, the largest increase by far in the military budget since the end of Cold War. In the fall of 2003, Bush signed a defense authorization bill for the following year of $401.3 billion.

Bush was guided by this approach as he prepared to go to war with Iraq in 2002. Iraq, he said, had developed weapons of mass destruction, and so was a menace to the region and the United States. The administration eventually

House of Representatives chamber

sought, but did not receive, approval of the United Nations for an attack on Iraq. With only one major ally, the Bush administration began its war against Iraq in March 2003. The Iraqi dictator Saddam Hussein was deposed after a couple of months and eventually captured, but one year after the war, hundreds of both Iraqis and American soldiers continued to be killed. The weapons of mass destruction that Bush feared had not been found, and in 2004, experts said they doubted that the weapons systems had ever existed.

__Preemptively__ has to do with taking the initiative (rather than waiting for others to act before responding).

The "War on Terrorism" that began after the attacks of September 11, 2001, also had a home front. The Bush administration pushed through a package of legislation collectively referred to as the USA Patriot Act. The legislative proposals that became this law were introduced less than a week after the attacks, and were signed into law on October 26, 2001. The act made significant amendments to more than fifteen important statutes, but was

Meeting of Senate Appropriations Committee

passed with little debate and with no House, Senate, or conference report.

Essentially, the act was a compromise version of the Anti-Terrorism Act of 2001, but it included new provisions that expand government ***investigative authority***, especially on the Internet. Other provisions deal with money laundering, bank procedures, wiretaps, and immigration. Russ Feingold, a Democrat and the only senator to oppose the act, said he opposed the law in part because it opened the immigrant community to abuse by expanded government authority.

But since its passage, the Patriot Act has come under criticism from a wide variety of sources. Librarians, for example, have objected to the provision that requires libraries to turn over book withdrawal records to the government. ***Civil libertarians*** have complained that the new law allows secret searches of property that are a radical departure from 4th Amendment standards.

Investigative authority is the power to gather information, sometimes in ways that might be considered to infringe on individual privacy.

Civil libertarians are people who support freedom from government interference, especially as guaranteed by the Bill of Rights.

One concrete reaction to the law has been a string of "resolutions" passed by communities across the country that deplore the Patriot Act. New York City, for example, in February 2004, became the 247th community in the country to oppose the legislation when the City Council deplored the law's infringement of privacy rights. The judicial branch has also criticized the law. In January 2004, a federal judge ruled that a provision of the Patriot Act violated the 1st and the 5th Amendments because it is too vague.

As the nation prepared to select another President in 2004, voters were as divided as they had ever been. Republicans and Democrats both expected a close and bitter fight for the top office.

Incumbents *are people who already occupy a political office.*

Despite this bitter rivalry, many voters don't participate in the system. For example, only a minority of qualified voters bothered to show up at the polls for the 1996 presidential election, the first time that had happened since 1924.

Analysis has shown that nonvoters are usually those people who benefit least from the American economy. Observers of modern American society also have observed a growing gap between the rich and the poor in this country over the last two decades. The Great Depression had the effect of leveling the differences in wealth among the population. In the decades that followed, the American economy in general recovered and the growth of the middle class grew. Recently, however, the income distribution has become more uneven.

The United States at the end of the twentieth century had the greatest levels of wealth inequality in its history. By 1999, the four hundred wealthiest Americans had increased their fortunes tenfold over the previous seventeen years. The top one percent of the population received 15.8 percent of the nation's income in 1997, as opposed to 9.3 percent in 1981. While the stock market boom of the 1990s enriched millions, the average after-tax income of the middle 60 percent of the population was lower than in 1977.

Many Americans viewed this growing gap between the wealthy and the rest of the population with alarm. Greater wealth allowed for greater political power, as elections became exceedingly expensive. In 1976, for example, Senate ***incumbents*** spent an average of $610,000 to keep their seats. By 2000, that figure had risen to $4.4 million, while the average winner in all Senate races raised $7.3 million.

THE
CONSTITUTION

Aside from the donations given by business, most of this money was raised from wealthy individuals. Twenty percent of the donors to the congressional election in 1997, for example, had incomes of $500,000 or more. Despite recent campaign reform legislation that finally passed Congress, the 2004 presidential contest was already shaping up to be the most expensive ever.

As we can see, the list of economic, political, and social problems facing the United States as the twenty-first century began is daunting—but the country has endured similar problems in its past.

The country survived and grew through its last period of income ***disparity*** during the "Gilded Age" at the end of the 1800s. In time, the national income tax and other progressive measures began to address the problem. And certainly no disparity is larger than the contrast of freedom and slavery. This bitter issue almost destroyed the nation, but the country emerging from the Civil War was stronger than ever.

And while civil rights may be under attack at the dawn of the twenty-first century, this period too has issues that are not new. Just seven years after the Bill of Rights was enacted, the Alien and Sedition Acts were passed, giving the President the power to ***deport*** aliens he deemed dangerous to the country. During the "Red Scare" early in the twentieth century, the federal government seemed to ignore the Bill of Rights as it pursued the Communists in this country.

Fifty years later, both the House Un-American Activities Committee and the investigations launched by Senator Joseph McCarthy trampled on the rights of Americans as the nation descended into a hysterical fear of Communists.

Joseph McCarthy, was a United States Republican Senator from the state of Wisconsin. An ardent anti-Communist, he led efforts

to hunt down Communist sympathizers in the military, government, and the entertainment industry. His campaign was discredited and the Senate voted 65 to 22 on December 2, 1954, to condemn McCarthy for "conduct that tends to bring the Senate into dishonor and disrepute."

In each of these cases, enough Americans in time believed in the country's founding principles—that all are created equal, and possess the right to life, liberty, and the pursuit of happiness—to ensure that these principles indeed did not vanish from this earth. There is no reason to think they will do so now.

*A **disparity** is a fundamental difference.*

***Deport** means to send a person back to his or her country of origin.*

September 11, 2001

Shortly before 8 A.M. on September 11, two Boeing 767 airplanes took off from Boston bound for Los Angeles. Both airplanes were hijacked shortly after take-off and redirected to New York City, where they were flown into the Twin Towers of the World Trade Center roughly one hour later.

At about 9:45, American Flight 77, which had flown out of Dulles International Airport in Washington D.C. and was also hijacked, was crashed into the Pentagon. At about 10:10, United Flight 93, which had departed from Newark, NJ, crashed in a wooded area of Pennsylvania after passengers resisted the hijackers on board.

The two World Trade Center towers collapsed roughly an hour after they were hit, killing hundreds of New York City policemen and firemen who were trying to rescue victims. All air traffic in the country was suspended, for the first time in history. The U.S. military was placed on high alert. The location of the U.S. President and the Vice President was kept secret for several hours.

By the end of the day, 2,752 were dead in New York, Pennsylvania, and Washington DC. The country had suffered billions of dollars of damage, but the most essential damage had no price tag. No longer could the United States harbor any illusions that it was immune from a catastrophic attack on its soil.

1215 British nobles force King John to sign the Magna Carta, considered the cornerstone of liberty and defense against unjust rule in England. The concessions establish for the first time the principle that government power can be limited by law.

July 4, 1776 The Declaration of Independence is approved by the Second Continental Congress in Philadelphia. Formal signing of the document began on August 2, 1776.

September 17, 1787 The U.S. Constitution is approved by Constitutional Convention.

1776 "Common Sense," by Thomas Paine, is published in Philadelphia. This influential pamphlet advocated democracy and independence for the British colonies of North America.

1765 The infamous Stamp Act is passed by the British Parliament. This law raised funds from the North American colonies by putting a tax on all official documents. All such documents had to carry an official "stamp," hence the name of the law. The law infuriated colonists and gave them one more reason to declare independence.

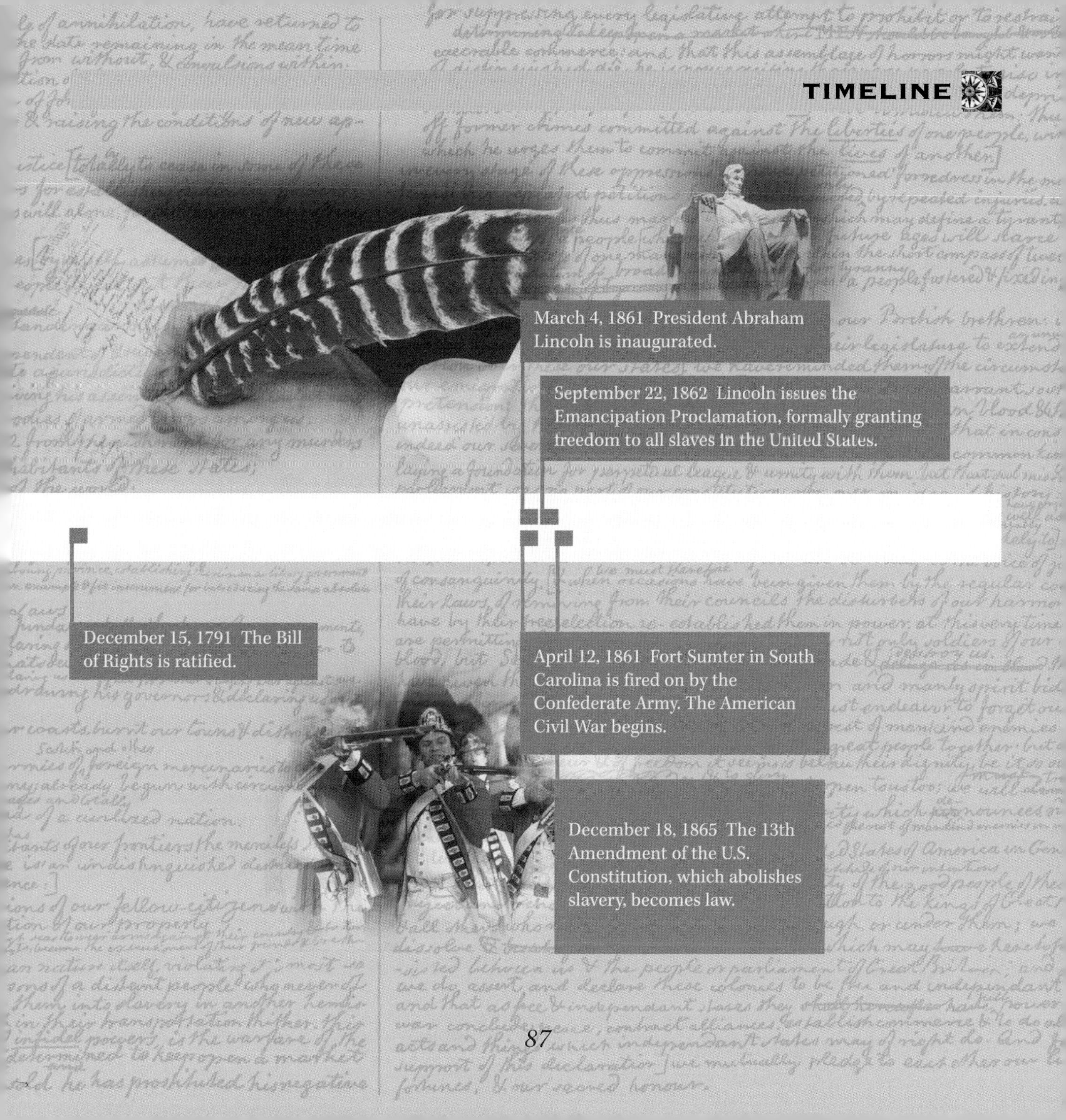

December 15, 1791 The Bill of Rights is ratified.

March 4, 1861 President Abraham Lincoln is inaugurated.

April 12, 1861 Fort Sumter in South Carolina is fired on by the Confederate Army. The American Civil War begins.

September 22, 1862 Lincoln issues the Emancipation Proclamation, formally granting freedom to all slaves in the United States.

December 18, 1865 The 13th Amendment of the U.S. Constitution, which abolishes slavery, becomes law.

July 9, 1868 The 14th Amendment, which was written to secure federal rights for freed slaves, is ratified.

February 3, 1870 The 15th Amendment, granting all citizens of the United States the right to vote, is ratified.

April 8, 1913 The 17th Amendment, which provides for the popular election of senators, is ratified.

August 18, 1920 The 19th Amendment, granting women the right to vote, is ratified.

October 29, 1929 "Black Tuesday" on Wall Street. Sometimes referred to as the unofficial beginning of the Great Depression in the United States.

April 4, 1968 Civil rights leader Martin Luther King Jr. is assassinated in Memphis, Tennessee.

October 26, 2001 USA Patriot Act is signed by President George W. Bush

January 23, 1964 The 23rd Amendment, which prohibits the use of poll taxes to restrict voting, is ratified.

September 11, 2001 Terrorist attacks in New York City, Pennsylvania, and Washington D.C. kill nearly 3,000 people.

FURTHER READING

Best, Judith. *The Choice of the People? Debating the Electoral College.* Lanham, Md.: Rowman & Littlefield Publishers, 1996.

Blackford, Mansel G. and K. Austin Kerr. *Business Enterprise in American History.* Boston: Houghton Mifflin, 1986.

Chafer, Byron E. and Anthony J. Badger, editors. *Contesting Democracy: Substance & Structure in American Political History, 1775–2000.* Lawrence: University Press of Kansas, 2001.

Donovan, Frank. *Mr. Jefferson's Declaration.* New York: Dodd, Mead & Co., 1998.

Hentoff, Nat. *Living the Bill of Rights: How to Be an Authentic American.* New York: HarperCollins, 1998.

Hirsh, Michael. *At War with Ourselves.* Oxford, U.K.: Oxford University Press, 2003.

Jennings, Francis. *The Creation of America.* Cambridge, U.K.: Cambridge University Press, 2000.

Longley, Lawrence D. and Neal R. Peirce. *The Electoral College Primer.* New Haven, Conn.: Yale Press, 1996.

Phillips, Kevin. *Wealth and Democracy.* New York: Random House, 2002.

Schumaker, Paul D. and Burdett A. Loomis. *Choosing a President.* New York: Chatham House Publishers, 2002.

Wood, Gordon S. *The Radicalism of the American Revolution.* New York: Alfred A. Knopf, 1992.

FOR MORE INFORMATION

National Archives
www.archives.gov/
Provides links to the Declaration of Independence, the U.S. Constitution, and the Bill of Rights.

Campaign Finance Information Center
www.campaignfinance.org/
Helps journalists follow the campaign money trail.

Contacting the Congress
www.visi.com/juan/congress/
Provides links to all senators and representatives.

The Federal Election Commission
www.fec.gov/
Gives information about the Electoral College and election procedures.

League of Women Voters
www.lwv.org/

U.S. Department of Commerce's Bureau of Economic Analysis
www.bea.doc.gov/

U.S. Department of State
usinfo.state.gov/usa/race/
Provides links to separate pages devoted to diversity in the United States and to civil rights.
usinfo.state.gov/topical/pol/terror/
Page on terrorism includes detailed information about the attacks of September 11, 2001.

U.S. House of Representatives
www.house.gov/

U.S. Senate
www.senate.gov/

The White House
www.whitehouse.gov/
Gives links to biographies of past Presidents and other historical information.

Publisher's note:
The Web sites listed on these pages were active at the time of publication. The publisher is not responsible for Web sites that have changed their addresses or discontinued operation since the date of publication. The publisher will review and update the Web sites upon each reprint.

INDEX

BIOGRAPHIES

AUTHOR

Eric Schwartz is a journalist living in Binghamton, New York. He received his bachelor's degree in Russian and journalism from Michigan State University and his master's degree in international relations from Syracuse University.

SERIES CONSULTANT

Dr. Jack N. Rakove is a professor of history and American studies at Stanford University, where he is director of American studies. The winner of the 1997 Pulitzer Prize in history, Dr. Rakove is the author of *The Unfinished Election of 2000, Constitutional Culture and Democratic Rule,* and *James Madison and the Creation of the American Republic.* He is also the president of the Society for the History of the Early American Republic.

PICTURE CREDITS

p. 1: National Archives and Records Administration
p. 8: Library of Congress,
pp. 8–9: Library of Congress
p. 11: Library of Congress
p. 12: Valley Forge Convention and Visitors Bureau
pp. 12–13: National Archives
p. 13: Left: National Archives; Right: Wildside
p. 14: Library of Congress
p. 15: Left: Photos.com; Right: Photos.com
p. 16: Left: Library of Congress; Right: PhotoSpiin
p. 17: Wildside
p. 18: Wildside
p. 19: Library of Congress
p. 20: Dover
p. 21: Library of Congress
p. 22: Boston Convention and Visitors Center
pp. 22–23: Library of Congress
p. 24: Corbis
p. 25: Left: Dover; Right: PhotoDisc
pp. 26–27: Photos.com
p. 27: PhotoDisc
p. 28: Library of Congress
p. 29: Left: Library of Congress; Right: Library of Congress
p. 30: National Archives and Records Administration
p. 31: WildSide
p. 32: Library of Congress
p. 34: Corbis
p. 35: Comstock
p. 36: Corbis
p. 37: PhotoDisc
p. 38: Dover
pp. 40—41: PhotoDisc
p. 42: Studio1
p. 43: National Archives and Records
p. 44: PhotoDisc
p. 46: Left: LBJ Library Photo by Yoichi R. Okamoto; Right: Library of Congress
p. 47: Department of the Interior
p. 48: Dover
p. 50: National Archives and Records Administration
p. 51: National Archives and Records Administration
p. 52: LBJ Library photo by O. J. Rapp
p. 53: National Archives and Records Administration
pp. 56–57: National Archives and Records Administration10
pp. 58–59: Comstock
pp.60–61: Comstock
p. 63: Dover
pp. 64–65: Dover
p. 66: Dover
p. 67: Dover
p. 70: National Archives and Records Administration
p. 71: National Archives and Records Administration
p. 72: Dover
pp. 72–73: PhotoDisc
p. 73: Photos.com
p. 74: Library of Congress
p. 75: Dwight D. Eisenhower Library
p. 76: Photos.com
p. 81: Dover
p. 82: Dover
p. 83: Dover
pp. 84–85: Photos.com
p. 86: Photos.com
p. 87: Top Left: Photospin; Bottom Left: Valley Forge Convention and Visitors Bureau; Right: PhotoDisc
p. 88: Top: PhotoDisc; Bottom: Library of Congress
p. 89: Top: National Archives and Records Administration; Bottom: PhotoDisc

FREE YAWF LEADERS
JAILED FOR AIDING
ANTI WAR G.I.
MP